corn snakes

understanding and
caring for your pet

Written by
Lance Jepson MA VetMB CBiol MSB MRCVS

Image by
© Peter Norby

corn snakes

understanding and
caring for your pet

Written by
Lance Jepson MA VetMB CBiol MSB MRCVS

Magnet & Steel Ltd

www.magnetsteel.com

ISBN: 978-1-907337-27-7
ISBN: 1-907337-27-X

Contents

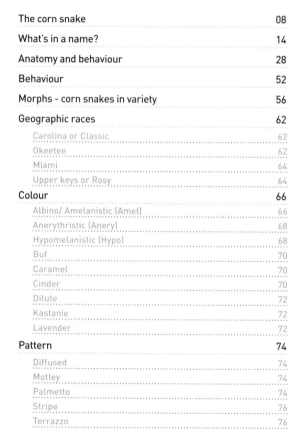

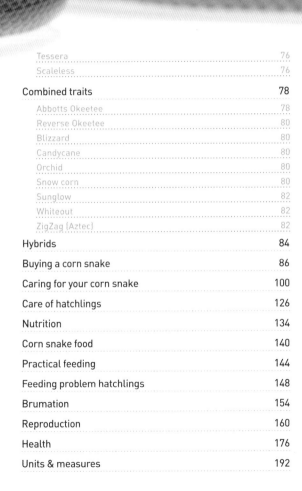

The corn snake

The corn snake (Pantherophis **guttatus**) is also known as the red corn **snake** or red rat snake. Whatever its **name**, the corn snake has much going for it as a pet. It is:

- Comparatively easy to keep

- Medium-sized (typically 76- 122cm/30- 48in)

- Readily tamed

- Attractively coloured

The original wild type has a glowing orange base colour with up to fifty or so red, black-bordered saddle-like patches repeated along the topside of the snake. However, if different colour morphs are your thing, the corn snake is available in pretty much any colour to suit your decor.

There is no need to feed live foods – pet corn snakes can be fed on commercially-produced, hygienic, mice that are now readily available frozen from local pet stores.

It is this preference for rodents that has helped give this snake its common name – corn snakes are often found around the corn and other grain stores of its native USA where it helps us by keeping down the rodent population.

The name may also refer to the markings on the underside of the corn snake that form an irregular checkerboard pattern reminiscent of maize or Indian corn. A popular pet, the corn snake has probably done more to redress the bad press given to snakes in the Bible than any other!

Life span

Wild corn snakes have many predators and so a 10-year life span would be considered a long (or lucky) one. But in captivity life spans of 20 to 25 years and more are possible.

Size

Corn snakes can vary in size depending upon their sex and their genetics. Males generally grow larger than females.

The largest males are usually around 122cm (4 feet) SVL (snout-vent length – the distance from the tip of the nose to the cloaca) but can grow to over 152cm (5 feet). These lengths are typical for most corn snakes except those from the Lower Keys in Florida. These are relatively diminutive, maxing out at around 76cm (30 in). Growth in reptiles continues throughout their lives although it slows down considerably with age. After around 5 years length will increase very little, although girth may continue to build.

Evolution

Snakes are thought to have evolved from a lizard-like ancestor sometime in the Jurassic period, 208 to 146 million years ago. The extreme changes in body form seen in snakes have given rise to two possible ideas about their evolutionary pathway. The most likely is that snakes spent a period of time as largely burrowing (fossorial) animals, rarely venturing above the surface. This would have coincided with the loss of limbs, the loss of eyelids, the marked elongation of the body with an increase in vertebral numbers, and the re-positioning of the internal organs into this new shape. One fossil species, Najash rionegrina, was discovered in totally terrestrial deposits in Argentina. This early snake has a pelvis attached to the spine and has fully functional limbs.

The internal structure of the eyes of modern snakes is different too from that of modern lizards and may have re-evolved when snakes resurfaced. The alternative hypothesis is that snakes entered an aquatic phase, and many of the anatomical changes could be considered adaptations to a life in water, although the evidence for this is less compelling.

Later the number of snake forms radiated out in line with a similar increase in mammals, their main prey. The early snakes were constrictors, and it is likely that the ancestors of modern corn snakes evolved during the Oligocene period, between 23 and 33 million years ago.

At a genetic level each of us vertebrate animals, be it corn snake, human or otherwise, possesses a series of genes that, in the developing embryo, dictate the types of vertebrae (backbones) that develop as well as the position of the limbs. These are known as the Hox genes. In snakes it seems that these Hox genes have altered so that the whole body from the first few vertebrae behind the skull down to the pelvic area are thorax-like rib-bearing backbones, an evolutionary dodge that has allowed them to develop such a versatile body form.

What's in a name?

Herpetologists of a certain age will know the corn snake as Elaphe guttata guttata. Today this beautiful snake has changed its name, and not for the first time. It is now known as Pantherophis guttatus. The genus Pantherophis was resurrected to distinguish the Elaphe rat snakes found north of Mexico from those assigned to the same genus in Europe and Asia. So the corn snake is now Pantherophis guttatus and has been since 2002...apart from a brief episode, between 2007 and 2008, when it was lumped into Pituophis, along with the other rat snakes.

At one time a complex of five different subspecies was suggested for the corn snake. These subspecies were:

- Elaphe guttata guttata (red corn snake).

- Elaphe guttata rosacea (rosy ratsnake).

- Elaphe guttata emoryi (great plains ratsnake).

- Elaphe guttata intermontanus.

- Elaphe guttata meahllmorum.

The reclassification of the corn snake means that the above subspecies classification seems reasonably well cleared up too – well, almost. A molecular study of corn snakes (Burbrink 2002) has now suggested that the corn snake is actually three species. These are:

1. Corn snake or red corn snake Pantherophis guttatus. This eastern form is the classic corn snake and is the subject of this book. It is native to the eastern and south-eastern United States. Corn snakes are found from southern New Jersey, Maryland and Kentucky southward to south-eastern Louisiana, southern Mississippi, southern Alabama, and southern Florida. It seems likely that the Mississippi river allowed speciation between this eastern form and the central form.

The corn snake was introduced to Grand Cayman Island around 1985. In addition it is found on Grand Bahama Island and may also be established elsewhere in the Caribbean region, such as St. Thomas, in the U.S. Virgin Islands. There are reports too from Curaco, Bonaire, Antigua, Anguilla, and St Barts. This eastern form includes the Rosy Ratsnake Elaphe guttata rosacea.

2. Slowinski's corn snake (Pantherophis slowinskii). This species represents a central form of the corn snake and is identified primarily by molecular techniques. It has a comparatively limited range that includes eastern Texas and western Louisiana, and possibly southern Arkansas.

3. Great plains or prarie ratsnake Pantherophis emoryi. The range of the great plains ratsnake extends from south-western Illinois, Missouri, southern South Dakota, and south-eastern Colorado southward to San Luis Potosi and Veracruz. It is found throughout Texas, with a separate population in eastern Utah and western Colorado. This species includes the types previously known as Elaphe guttata intermontanus and E.g. meahllmorum.

The above classification will be used in this book. Other North American ratsnakes are also now included in Patherophis.

These include Baird's rat snake (Pantherophis bairdi), yellow-red rat snake (P. flavirufus), eastern fox snake (P. gloydi), eastern ratsnake (P. obsoletus) and the western fox snake (P. vulpinus).

Corn snakes belong to the family Colubridae, subfamily Colubrinae. Colubrid snakes are the most diverse group of snakes and are found on every continent apart from Antarctica and the oceanic islands.

Natural history and ecology

Corn snakes like plenty of cover, partly to increase their feelings of security, and because that is where their prey lives. Hence they prefer wooded areas, especially mature upland pine forests on sand or loam soils, but oakwoods are also inhabited. Here there is a great variety of fallen trunks, stumps and rotten logs to provide cover both for the snake and its food. There is usually a water source nearby such as a pond or stream. Ever adaptable however, Lower Keys populations are also found in mangrove forests.

Zappalorti (2011) records an average activity range of 15.77 hectares (43.91 acres) in a study of eleven free-ranging corn snakes in Ocean County and Cumberland County, New Jersey. The actual ranges varied from 6.82 hectares to 59.07 hectares (16.86 acres to 145.96 acres). In this same study it was found that wild corn snakes spend a great deal of time (estimated at around 55%) hidden away in underground hides such as fissures in rocks and rodent burrows. They spend over half the rest of their time hidden beneath surface objects such as leaf litter and rotten bark that had fallen from logs. This is especially true of smaller corn snakes and hatchlings, which tend to prefer the sunnier aspects of these logs, as do their prey species of skinks and anoles.

They are active and visible above surface for less than 20% of their time, when they undertake necessary behaviours such as foraging, eating, drinking, basking, mating, shedding or resting.

They are often found close to human habitation, such as barns and abandoned buildings, where there are abundant small mammals and birds. In one study (Sperry and Taylor 2008) great plains ratsnakes (P. emoryi) were shown to prefer areas with more structure, such as trees, ground cover and man-made rock structures used to control soil erosion. They can also be found under human debris such as discarded rubbish. Corn snakes are also excellent climbers and will take eggs and fledglings from nests, as well as adult birds. Corn snakes are proficient swimmers too.

Adult corn snakes are primarily rodent predators, although they will take other similar-sized prey such as small birds and bats. Hatchling corn snakes will initially begin to feed on small lizards, amphibians such as frogs, and even caterpillars, before graduating on to rodents as their size, and ability to overcome larger creatures, increases. In Florida, corn snakes prey on the abundant numbers of small reptiles such as brown anoles (Anolis sagrei) and house geckos (Hemidactylus sp).

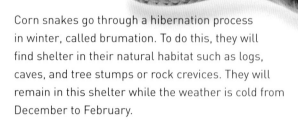

Corn snakes go through a hibernation process in winter, called brumation. To do this, they will find shelter in their natural habitat such as logs, caves, and tree stumps or rock crevices. They will remain in this shelter while the weather is cold from December to February.

Reproduction

Wild corn snakes become sexually mature at two to three years of age. Sexual maturity in reptiles is size-dependant rather than age-related and typically these snakes will be around 100cm (39in) in length by that time. The females will lay between 3 and 40 eggs in a clutch, with an average of around 14. In North Carolina this is usually in June or July and typically only one clutch is laid. Some females may not breed every year.

Predators

A wide variety of predators, great and small, are a threat to wild corn snakes of all ages, including their eggs. These include black bear, coyote, fox, skunk, nine-banded armadillo, feral pigs, dogs and cats. There are also a number of snake-eating (ophiophagus) snakes that will prey on adults, hatchlings and eggs.

These are indigo snakes Drymarchon spp, king snakes Lampropeltis spp, black racers Coluber constrictor, coachwhips Masticophis spp and scarlet snakes Cemophora coccinea. In certain areas introduced fire ants will kill hatching snakes. Wild corn snakes caught in the open will often freeze when scared, which is probably why many are also killed on the roads by traffic, particularly in spring and autumn when corn snakes are more diurnal (Dodd et al 1989).

Picture:
Armadillo

Conservation

Globally the population of corn snakes is secure and the IUCN list it as of Least Concern. However, locally it can be threatened and has been considered Endangered in New Jersey since 1984 due to habitat loss and over-collection for the pet trade. Here the collection or possession of wild corn snakes is prohibited by the New Jersey Endangered Species Act and is punishable with fines and imprisonment. In Florida the Lower Keys population is listed as a Species of Special Concern.

References

Burbrink, F.T. (2002). Phylogeographic analysis of the cornsnake (Elaphe guttata) complex as inferred from maximum likelihood and Bayesian analyses. Molecular Phylogenetics and Evolution 25 465–476.

Dodd C.K., Enge K.M and Stuart J.N. Reptiles on Highways in North-Central Alabama, USA. Journal of Herpetology, Vol. 23, No. 2, pp. 197-200.

Keogh J.S. (1996) Evolution of the Colubrid Snake Tribe Lampropeltini: A Morphological Perspective. Herpetologica 52(3) 406-416.

Parmley, D. and Lacy G. (1997) Holocene Herpetofauna of the Box Elder Creek Local Fauna, Caddo County, Oklahoma. Journal of Herpetology, Vol 31, No. 4, pp. 624-625.

Sperry J.H. and Taylor C.A. (2008) Habitat use and seasonal activity patterns of the Great Plains Ratsnake (Elaphe guttata emoryi) in central Texas. The Southwestern Naturalist 53(4): 444-449.

Utiger, U. Helfenberger N., Schätti, B. Schmidt, C., Ruf, M. and Ziswiler, V. (2002) Molecular Systematics and Phylogeny of Old and New World Ratsnakes, Elaphe Auct, and Related Genera (Reptilia, Squamata, Colubridae). Russian Journal of Herpetology, Vol 9, No 2, pp 105-124.

Zappalorti R. (2011) Supplemental Information for the Red Rat Snake (Lower Keys Population) Biological Status Review Report. Florida Fish and Wildlfie Conservation Commission.

Anatomy and behaviour

We all know what a snake looks like. A corn snake is a beautiful animal, and it is also a miracle of evolution. So, what defines a snake? The main characteristic is a tubular body-form, and, as part of this package there is a loss of limbs (limblessness), a greatly increased number of backbones (vertebrae) and an increase in skull flexibility.

Tubular body-form

Snakes have evolved into elongated, tubular-shaped animals – basically a long thorax of ribbed backbones (vertebrae) that is both very strong and very flexible. Adopting this body shape has also led to some rearrangement of the internal organs. These include:

- Marked modification of the respiratory system. The trachea (wind-pipe) is very long and supported by complete cartilaginous rings that protect the airway while the snake swallows its prey. There is only one lung – the right. The left lung is hardly present at all (vestigial). The right lung is elongated and extends along much of the body length of the snake. The first third or so of the lung is supplied with many blood vessels, and it is here that oxygen take-up and carbon dioxide release occurs. The rest of the lung is more of an air-sac that is used to shuttle air backwards and forwards through the first third between breaths. Snakes cannot cough.

- The right kidney lies in front of the left, instead of opposite it.

- The right ovary is in front of the left ovary in females.

- There is no urinary bladder.

Increased backbone number

The number of back bones (vertebrae) that make up the whole spinal column is dramatically increased. Corn snakes have some 315 vertebrae. Most of these are rib-bearing and it is this characteristic that gives snakes their flexibility and strength.

Limblessness

Corn snakes have no arms or legs, but they can move in several different ways. There are four types of snake locomotion known as serpentine, concertina, side-winding and rectilinear. Serpentine motion involves sending the body into a series of alternating curves, bracing the body against the ground and moving so that all parts of the body faithfully follow the head and neck.

In confined spaces, such as burrows, snakes can use concertina movement where the body wall is thrown into a series of curves so that the outermost crest is in contact with the surface. This presents a fixed point against which the rest of the snake can be pulled.

When side-winding, only parts of the body are kept in contact with the surface and progress at an angle to the forward movement. This is a surprisingly energy efficient form of transportation.

Rectilinear motion involves a wave of rib movements that propel the snake forward. This form of movement is usually only seen in the larger snakes, such as boas and pythons.

Skull flexibility

The snake skull is lightly built and can flex at several points. There is a fallacy that a snake can dislocate its jaw. In reality the jaw joint is not a simple hinge joint, as it is with humans. Instead, there are three bones involved – the supratemporal, the quadrate and the mandible, so that there are two joints in total on each side. In addition the two jawbones (mandibles) are not joined together at the front, but instead have a stretchy ligamentar attachment. All of these adaptations have the effect of increasing the gape by two to three times – impressive, but it cannot stop there. Having no limbs means no arms or hands to guide or push food into the mouth, nor anything with which to hold food in order to tear it into bite-sized chunks.

The snake has solved this problem with two neat adaptations. The first is by developing an extra set of teeth. All teeth in a snake are backward-pointing. They have a single set of teeth on the lower jaw (maxilla), but two sets on the upper (pterygoid and palatine sets).

The second is the increased skull flexibility that means that left and right sides can be moved backward and forward independently. Once prey is in the mouth those backward-pointing rows of teeth mean that it is going nowhere.

First one side of the mouth, then the other, is advanced and bears down on to the prey, which is gripped and then pulled back so that gradually, millimetre by millimetre, the prey is ratcheted into the mouth and down into the gullet of the snake.

The skin of a snake is not necessarily what it seems. The scales are not distinct plates as they are in fish, but are thickenings of the outer skin layer – the epidermis – with thinner areas of skin between. Although this is common to all reptiles, in the snake this type of skin has one huge advantage – stretchiness. When swallowing prey that is often of a greater diameter than the snake, everything must distend to accommodate this, including the skin, which stretches at the thinner sections between the scales.

Snakes, like all reptiles, shed their skin regularly as part of the process of growth and maintenance, a process under hormonal control. As with lizards, the skin is shed simultaneously across the whole body, but unlike lizards it should all come away as one continuous sheet. This shedding is known as ecdysis and in snakes it also includes both of the spectacles over the eye.

At a microscopic level skin shedding involves the following stages, and these are reflected in what we actually see with the snake:

1. A resting phase. This is the normal state of the skin between sheds. Microscopically there is an outer thickened layer that consists of the skin and scales, with a thin growth layer beneath it.

2. When a shed is imminent the growth layer begins to proliferate. There is no outward visible change in the snake.

3. The proliferation begins to formalize into a new thickened layer beneath the old outer one. This produces an increase in the thickness of the skin, which we can begin to see as a slight dulling of the skin colours; the spectacle may appear slightly cloudy.

4. By the time the newly-produced inner thickened layer is properly developed, a thin intermediate layer has formed between the two thick layers. The skin is at its maximum thickness now and so the snake's colours are at their dullest and the spectacle is obviously cloudy.

5. The intermediate layer is then dissolved, separating the outer and inner thicker layers to form a cleavage plane.

The loss of this layer means that snake's colours will be seen to brighten and the spectacle will clear.

6. Approximately four to seven days after the spectacles clear, the old outer thickened layer is shed, usually in one or two pieces.

The snake will begin the shedding process by rubbing its nose against rough surfaces to break the old skin at the areas of the mouth and jaw. Once the skin is broken the snake will then rub against rough or firm surfaces so that it can gradually work its way out of the old skin. During this process the old skin becomes turned back and may bunch into folds. Eventually the snake will work itself free of the shed skin. At this point the colours of your snake will be at their most stunning.

Baby snakes will normally shed around seven to fourteen days or so after hatching. The skin of hatchling corn snakes is chemically different to that of older snakes (Ball 2004) and is thought to be more fluid-permeable and therefore more suitable for life inside the egg. Once outside, the skin is replaced by a less permeable one. In fact they will undergo a shed of sorts while in the egg, some five to six days before hatching.

If well fed, a corn snake hatchling will shed some 6 to 8 times during its first year. Once adult size is reached, this will reduce to 2 to 4 times per year. Shedding is a function of growth and so the rate of shedding depends upon a number of environmental factors, such as frequency of feeding and whether the snake undergoes brumation or not.

Special senses

Corn snakes have reasonably good vision. They have no eyelids. Instead, the eye is protected by a spectacle or brille – a transparent scale which derives embryologically from the eyelids. Tears are produced and flow into the space between the spectacle and the cornea, keeping the eye lubricated and cleansed. Snakes focus by moving their lens backwards or forwards in the eye, unlike lizards and us humans that deform the lens to alter its optical properties. Corn snakes can see in the ultraviolet, which may help in detecting prey trails as well as selecting appropriate basking areas.

Snakes do not have an external ear – probably an adaptation to a burrowing, below-ground phase of their evolution – but they do have a fully-functional inner ear.

This ear is connected by a series of bones to the lower jaw and so vibrations, even the tiniest footfalls of rodents, can be detected by this arrangement if the snake rests its jaws on to the substrate (Friedel 2008). The fact that the two jawbones are only connected by ligaments means that each jaw is relatively free of vibrational interference from the other jaw. The result is that snakes can hear differentially between the sides so that functionally they hear in stereo – something they can use to help locate prey or potential threats. Rattlesnakes have been shown to be able to hear air-borne sounds (Young and Aguiar, 2002) so it is likely that your corn snake can too. Therefore not only can snakes hear, they can hear in stereo and they have two different means of doing so.

Corn snakes have three means of sensing food and other chemicals. These are olfaction (sense of smell) detected in the lining of the nose; gustation (taste) detected in the lining of the tongue and other oral surfaces; vomerolfaction detected in the lining of specialised vomeronasal organs situated in the roof of the mouth. Vomerolfaction picks up non-airborne scent particles from the tongue and lining of the mouth, and may play a part not only in food detection but also individual recognition based on a given snake's scent profile.

This may apply as much to how your corn snake recognises you as it does to how it tells other snakes apart. Tongue-flicking is used to pick up these scent particles, either from the air or from surfaces. Also, newly -hatched corn snakes have been shown to react positively to mouse odour by significantly increasing the number of tongue flicks (which brings into play their vomerolfaction). They also respond to snake scents and will avoid shelters that previously housed other snakes.

The forked tongue is a piece of anatomy that many people instantly attribute to a snake. The tongue is also the most expressive part of the snake's head and is used in a variety of functions and displays, as listed below by Gove and Burghart (1983).

• **Exploration**. Snakes find out a great deal about their environment, including the presence of prey, by vomerolfaction. During exploration the snake tongue oscillates slowly (with first an upward then a downward swing of the tongue); a relatively large area of the tongue is exposed and can be of long duration, possibly either to scan their surroundings or concentrate low-level scent particles. Explorational tongue-flicks may be triggered by environmental changes such as vibrations, touching or new objects appearing in sight.

- **Trailing and feeding.** In snakes that are following a prey trail tongue flicks are rapid with short extensions. Scent particles are probably present at high levels and rapid flicking may provide constant real-time upgrading of important information, such as nearness of non-visible prey. Once a prey is sighted then, again, tongue flicking is rapid.

- **Individual recognition.** Corn snakes introduced to each other may show slow tongue flicks with maximum tongue extension, probably to gain as much information as possible. Arguably this is a form of exploration.

- **Defensive.** Each time the tongue is protruded from the mouth it oscillates several times at long extension. The oscillations are slow and deliberate and, combined with the obvious long tongue, serve as a ritualised warning display.

Feeding

Corn snakes are constrictors. Feeding snakes can be highly variable in the position they adopt when constricting, the amount of muscular activity they use and the force they exert. Typically, they invoke sideways bends of the front part of the body to wind themselves into a vertical coil around the prey.

Three common constriction postures are fully encircling loops that form a coil, partially encircling loops, and non-encircling loops that pinion the prey. Initial tightening of a coil occurs by winding or pressing the loops tighter to reduce the diameter of the coil.

The most common belief is that constricting snakes subdue their prey with asphyxiation – by enveloping in a series of coils that prevent the prey animal from breathing. However, measuring the pressures generated during constriction by snakes of a similar size to corn snakes (gopher snake Pituophis melanoleucus and king snake Lampropeltis getula) showed pressures of over half to twice a mouse's maximum blood pressure is exerted on their small mammal prey. Such high pressures probably kill by inducing immediate circulatory and cardiac arrest, rather than by suffocation alone.

Snakes can probably differentiate between live and dead prey before striking, and it seems that factors other than body temperature and movement influence the attack and prey handling strategies. Snakes do appear to assess the activity levels of their prey, size and strength before striking and will adjust how they will deal with their prey beforehand (Moon 2000).

Vomerolfaction may also be important, with snakes tongue flicking their prey before capture. They respond most actively to muscle movements by tightening their coils, but also react to breathing and heartbeat. Coil formation is quicker and lasts longer with live prey than it does with dead.

In one interesting study (Heinrich and Klaasen, 1985) some snakes were shown to have left or right-sided dominance when coiling around prey – that is to say that they exhibited a preference for whether the left or right side of their body was pressed against the prey. In other words, some snakes were left or right 'handed'. Two great plains rat snakes Pantherophis (Elaphe guttata) emoryi were included in this study and showed a tendency towards right-handedness. Also when these snakes attempted to constrict the opposite way they appeared slow and awkward. One eastern rat snake (P. obsoletus) failed to subdue its prey this way and was bitten too!

Once their prey is dead the snake will begin to manipulate it so that it is swallowed head first, using a number of tactile cues to tell it which way to go, such as hair or feather direction. Smaller items may be swallowed either way; larger may be released and the snake will reposition it if it is going down the wrong way.

Digestion time is temperature dependant – indeed, if the temperature is too low, digestion does not occur and the snake may regurgitate. At a body temperature of 26°C (78.8°F) it takes around 3 days to fully digest a meal (from consumption to defaecation) whilst at 18- 20°C (64.4- 68°F) it is around 5 to 8 days.

Reptiles excrete their metabolic waste nitrogen, not as urea as we do, but as uric acid crystals – this is the white sand-like sludgy substance naturally present in their urine. Note that this is not calcium, as many people believe. Reptiles attempt to save water and by excreting uric acid as a sludge they need lose less water as urine than by eliminating urea, a substance that requires relatively large volumes of water in which to dissolve and to carry it. Snakes do not have a urinary bladder. The kidneys are paired structures situated one in front of the other. Urine is formed here and is drained down the ureters into the cloaca. Reptile kidneys cannot concentrate urine, so this is further concentrated by having water absorbed by refluxing urine back into the large intestine.

As with all reptiles, corn snakes do not have separate external orifices for the urinogenital tract and bowel; instead they have a cloaca, which is a chamber into which the gut, urinary tract and reproductive tract all communicate.

This intermingling of excreta is largely why corn snakes often produce urine and faeces at the same time. The entrance to the cloaca is ventrally at the base of the tail and is marked by a slit-like opening.

Reproduction

Corn snakes are oviparous – they lay eggs.
Female corn snakes have two ovaries, with the
right ovary always in front of the left ovary. The
female reproductive cycle can be divided into four
phases, which occur one after the other (Aldridge et
al 2009). These are:

1. **Vitellogenesis.** The yolk is synthesised in the
   liver and transported to the ovaries. It begins in
   the Spring, once the snake revives from brumation,
   and takes some 5 to 7 weeks. In wild corn snakes
   vitellogenesis occurs in May and June, without
   courtship or mating.

2. **Attractiveness.** This is when the female is
   attractive to males, both by her behaviour and
   certain physical attributes, such as pheromone
   production. Female snakes produce a sex
   pheromone contained in the skin lipids. This is
   released after a post-hibernation skin shed and
   makes her irresistible to male corns!

3. **Ovulation.** The female germinative cells along
   with the yolks are released from the ovaries into
   the oviduct, where they are fertilised and covered
   by the shell to form an egg.

4. **Oviposition,** or egg-laying.

Image by
© Mark Leppin

The mating season is the time of year when females in a population are likely to come into oestrus. In corn snakes, as with most but not all North American snakes, it is the spring. Some females may not breed every year.

Male corn snakes have two testes. In addition, male snakes have an extra section attached to the kidney, known as the sexual segment. This produces secretions needed for mating, in particular the seminal or copulatory plug. When produced, this is a gelatinous mass full of spermatozoa that is introduced into the female during mating and it blocks the female's oviduct. This plug both prevents other males from mating successfully, and contains pheromones which reduce the female's attractiveness. This plug can last from 2 to 14 days, dependant upon temperature. Sperm production by males occurs during the summer after mating and is stored over winter in the testes and associated structures.

Males have two intromittant organs – the hemipenes- which function like a penis during mating. When not in use they lie in two ventral pockets along the underside of the tail caudal to the cloaca.

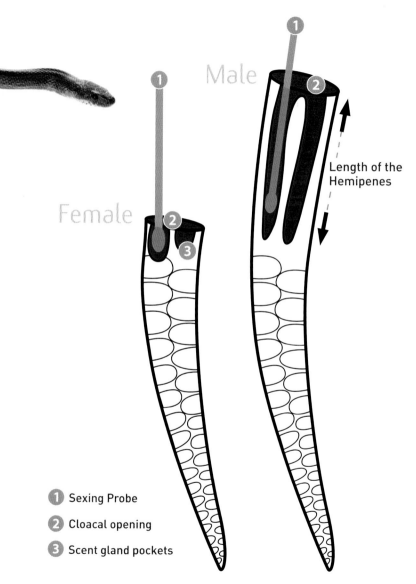

Female

Male

Length of the Hemipenes

1. Sexing Probe
2. Cloacal opening
3. Scent gland pockets

Behaviour

Learning

Corn snakes are highly evolved animals, perfectly adapted for their lifestyle, yet many people think of them as unintelligent. It is true that much of their behaviour is instinctive, but snakes can learn, providing what they learn is relevant to being a snake. As an example, young corn snakes were shown to have spatial awareness and memory as they were able to learn where a shelter was, choosing the one out of eight identical holes that gave access to the shelter (Holtzman et al 1999). After 4 days they moved more quickly and more directly to it, making less errors than chance would suggest. We know that corn snakes spend half their time hidden, so gaining the comparative safety of a shelter would be something important to a corn snake.

Caudal distraction

Corn snakes, particularly hatchlings and young, will rapidly vibrate their tail in an erratic, whip-like fashion. In the eastern ratsnake (P. obsoletus) this behaviour has been shown to increase the prey capture rate of the snake, possibly by distracting the prey rodent's attention away from the approaching head. The snake will usually start vibrating its tail as it approaches its prey, but before the prey is within strike range.

References

Aldridge R.D., Goldberg S.R., Wisniewshi S.S, Bufalino A.P. and Dillan C.B. (2009) The reproductive cycle and estrus in the colubrid snakes of temperate North America. Contemporary Herpetology 2009.1-31.

Ball J.C. (2004). The First Shed Skin of Neonate Corn Snakes Is Chemically Different from Adult Shed Skins. Journal of Herpetology, Vol. 38, No. 1, pp. 124-127.

Bruce A. Young B.A, and Aguiar A. (2002) Response of western diamondback rattlesnakes Crotalus atrox to airborne sounds. The Journal of Experimental Biology 205, 3087–3092 .

Friedel P., Young B.A. , and van Hemmen J.L. (2008) Auditory Localization of Ground-Borne Vibrations in Snakes. Phys. Rev. Lett. 100, 048701 (2008).

Gove D. and Burghardt G.M. (1983) Context-correlated parameters of snake and lizards tongue-flicking, Animal Behaviour. 31, 718-723.

Heinrich M.L and Klaassen H.E. (1985) Side Dominance in Constricting Snakes. Journal of Herpetology, Vol. 19, No. 4, pp. 531-533.

Holtzamn D.A., Harris T.W., Aranguren G. and Bostock E. (1999) Spatial learning of an escape task by young corn snakes, Elaphe guttata guttata. Animal Behaviour, vol 57, 51–60.

Moon B.R. (2000) The mechanics and muscular control of constriction in gopher snakes (Pituophis melanoleucus) and a king snake (Lampropeltis getula). J. Zool., Lond. (2000) 252, pp 83-98.

Morphs— corn snakes in variety

One of the most fascinating aspects of keeping corn snakes is the sheer range of colours and patterns available as a result of years of selective breeding by hobbyists and commercial breeders alike. If there is such a thing as the domestic snake (like our domestic dog or domestic cat), then the captive-bred corn snake is it.

The majority of the corn snake varieties, usually referred to as morphs, are the result of distinct non-life-threatening genetic changes that cause alterations in colour or pattern. Some morphs are created by combining multiple variations into individual snakes.

These are sometimes known as designer morphs and they can be expensive to buy.

Some breeders favour a classification of corn snake morphs based upon the number and type of genetic changes that create each morph. Snakes, at the moment of conception, receive two copies (known as alleles) of each gene needed to create a new corn snake – one from each parent. How these alleles interact with each other can vary and, where they are involved with colouring or pattern, they can dictate the final appearance of the snake. Therefore morphs may be described as:

- **Single dominant.** These morphs are the result of a single genetic change, and are said to be dominant because the different appearance is still present when only one altered copy of the gene (i.e. from one parent only) is present.

- **Single recessive.** Again, due to a single genetic abnormality, but it is recessive because it will be masked if a normal or wild-type copy of the gene is present. Therefore the changes it encodes for will not be apparent unless the snake has two abnormal copies of the gene i.e. one from each parent. Snakes with only one altered copy of the gene appear normal, but carry the potential to transmit the gene into the next generation.

Such snakes are referred to as heterozygous, which is normally shortened to het. Sometimes they are called split instead. Therefore a normal-looking snake known to carry one gene for albinism will be referred to as het or split for albino. The term simple recessive, as used in this book, means that the gene passes into the next generation as you would expect by standard Mendelian genetics.

- **Codominant.** This usually refers to when two genes, each of which would normally produce a certain morph, combine to give a third, different morph. Actually what is referred to as codominance in reptile literature is often an example of incomplete dominance – true codominance is where both genes are expressed and visible simultaneously. In other words, the offspring will show the characteristics of both parents. Compare this with incomplete dominance, which produces a snake with an appearance very different from its parents.

- **Double trait morphs are the result of two genetic variations.** For example, one may be giving a particular colour, while the other a certain pattern. Triple trait morphs need three gene mutations to produce them, and so on.

- **Lines.** These are where snakes of a particular general type or form have been selectively bred to enhance that appearance. Many genes are involved. Line-bred Okeetee corns would be examples of this.

There is a bewildering array of corn snake morphs available –well over 200 different morphs have been documented – so this books offers an alternative way of classification based upon four different categories of variation. These are:

- Geographic race

- Colour

- Pattern

- Physical (structural)

Geographic races

The geographic races are the least well-defined types because corn snakes are naturally so variable in appearance. In truth, the stated characteristics that are said to define each race represent an average for the typical appearance of corn snakes in that area. Unlike most true morphs they are not the result of genetic mutations.

Carolina or Classic corn snake

This is the orange corn snake with red dorsal markings edged with black.

Okeetee corn snake

This is considered by many to be the definitive corn snake in appearance, with a bright orange body colour overlaid with high-contrast, black-lined red markings.

Top:
Carolina Corn snake

Bottom:
Okeetee Corn Snake

The Okeetee corn snake takes its name from the Okeetee Plantation and Hunt Club in Jasper County, South Carolina. Corn snakes from this area were brought to the attention of the reptile-keeping world by the herpetologist and author Carl Kauffeld during the 1960s, especially in his 1969 book Snakes: The Keeper and the Kept, with it's chapter Life and Death on Okeetee. However, snakes matching typical Okeetee can be found along the entire Atlantic range from North Carolina down to northern Florida. Corn snakes that form part of the native Okeetee populations may not be quite so handsome. Selective breeding of lines from original Okeetee snakes has produced some stunning snakes.

Miami

These corn snakes from northern Florida tend to have a more grey background that contrasts with dark to bright red, black-lined markings.

Upper keys or rosy

A smaller geographic race from the Florida Keys, this corn has heightened reds and often a hypomelanistic appearance. Previously considered a separate subspecies Elaphe gutatta rosecea.

Pictured:
Miami Corn Snake

Colour

Albino/Amelanistic (Amel)

Albinism is a lack of the black pigment called melanin, and therefore this condition affects only black and similar colours that are made by the same biochemical pathways. Hence these snakes lack any black or brown, but can still show reds and yellows; typically the eyes are red or ruby too. The red markings are vibrant as there is no overlying black to mask the colouring, and they are contrasted in the most vivid fashion by white borders (which are black in normal corns) on an orange body. Often called Red Albino because these snakes are very red, but it is probably more appropriately known as Amelanistic (shortened to Amel). This describes the snake's lack of black pigment and implies that other pigments are still present. It is a simple recessive gene. The Amel gene is truly codominant with the Ultra gene (Hypo type D) so that when a snake has one of each gene, an intermediate appearance known as Ultramel is seen.

Pictured:

Albino/ Amelanistic Corn Snake

Anerythristic (Anery)

This is a lack of red pigment. There are two distinct genes that can cause this:

- **Aneryththristic Type A.** Known also by the confusing term of black albino, this produces a snake patterned in greys and blacks. Older Type A's may develop some yellow pigment on the throat and neck, and the greys may darken to a brown. It is a simple recessive.

- **Anerythristic Type B.** These are known as charcoal albinos and in appearance are almost identical to Type A, although they may lack the yellow colouring. However they are different genes. It is a simple recessive.

Hypomelanistic (Hypo)

Hypomelanistics, or Hypos, show a reduction in the amount of black pigmentation. Five different types have been identified in corn snakes.

- **Hypo Type A.** These snakes have reduced black markings, heightening the appearance of the oranges and yellows. It is a recessive gene that is said to be codominant with strawberry.

- **Hypo Type B (sunkissed).** These snakes have reduced black, which gives very brightly-coloured snakes. Simple recessive.

Top:
Anerythristic
Corn snake

Bottom:
Hypomelanistic
Corn Snake

- **Hypo Type C (Lava).** This gene has a more pronounced effect on the black than other Hypo genes and is a simple recessive.

- **Hypo Type D (Ultra).** This is a simple recessive that is codominant with Amel.

- **Strawberry.** A fairly new gene isolation, it is a recessive gene that is said to be codominant with Hypo Type A.

Buf

This gene has a hypoerythrystic effect, reducing the red colouration. It is a dominant gene.

Caramel

Red pigment is minimal in this type, producing a snake in light browns and yellows. It is a simple recessive.

Cinder

Also known as Ashy, Morph Z or just Z. This affects the reds and yellows, producing a snake with dark burgundy patterns on a grey body. It is a recessive gene.

Pictured:

*Caramel
Corn Snake*

Dilute

This causes a pronounced and progressive loss of colour as the snake ages, almost as if the snake is constantly in shed. A recessive gene.

Kastanie

Named after the German word for chestnut, hatchling kanasties appear like anerythristics but develop darker brown and orange tones as they mature. A recessive gene.

Lavender

As these snakes age the skin tones become a pale grey with pinkish highlights and lavender-coloured blotches. The eyes are ruby-coloured. A recessive gene.

Pictured:

Lavender
Corn Snake

Pattern

Diffused

This gene causes a disruption and progressive loss of the pattern on the sides of the snake and a loss of the black chequers on the underside. A recessive gene. Another gene – pied – may be linked to the diffused gene. This gene causes random patches of white along the sides.

Motley

This gene causes the blotches and saddles to merge into each other randomly. On occasion, striped and partially-striped snakes result. A recessive gene, it is however dominant to stripe.

Palmetto

A very different corn snake in appearance and, at the time of writing, extremely rare. They are white (including the iris) with a random scattering of coloured scales along the body. A recessive gene.

Pictured:

Motley
Corn Snake

Stripe

The dorsal pattern is altered into two parallel horizontal stripes along the whole length of the snake's body. There are two finer stripes on the sides. A recessive gene. Some lines of stripe have been line-bred to reduce the amount of pattern progressively, they are termed "patternless" or "vanishing stripe".

Terrazzo

Snakes with this gene develop a pattern similar to stripe at the first part of the body that then deteriorates in a flecked, granite-like pattern. Recessive gene.

Tessera

A new morph which gives corn snakes a garter snake-like pattern. There are dorsal stripes that extend the full length of the body, while the sides have chequered markings. The ventral pattern is reduced. This is a dominant gene.

Physical

Scaleless

This morph has dramatically reduced scalation to give a smooth, velvety appearance. Believed to be a recessive gene, Scaleless corns are rare.

Top:
Stripe
Corn Snake

Bottom:
Scalelss
Corn Snake

Combined traits

With selective breeding, examples of all four categories can be combined into a given corn snake. Some particularly attractive combinations of colours and patterns have been selectively bred for and have been given their own names. These morphs are sometimes referred to as designer morphs, a name that reflects as much their expense as it does their rarity. The number of such morphs is huge with more being created every year. Some of the more popular or interesting ones are:

Abbotts Okeetee

A line-bred Okeetee with the high reds and oranges but selected for wide black margins around the dorsal markings.

Pictured:
Abbotts Okeetee
Corn Snake

Reverse Okeetee

An amelanisitc version of the Okeetee; same bright reds and oranges but the black markings are replaced with white.

Blizzard

An almost completely white snake, with only faint markings. This morph is a combination of amelanistic and charcoal (anerythristic Type B).

Candycane

A line of amelanistics bred to have enhanced red and yellow markings on a bright white background. Some yellowish markings develop on the neck as the snake ages.

Orchid

This snake is coloured with delicate pastel shades of pink, orange and blue. It is a combination of lavender and sunkissed (Hypo Type B).

Snow corn

A popular morph, this corn snake develops into a white corn with pale yellow markings. It is a combination of amelanistic and anerythristic (probably Type A), leaving only the yellow pigmentation behind.

From top:
Candycane
Reverse Okeetee
Blizzard
Snow Corn

Sunglow

A line of amelanistics bred to reduce the amount of white patterning to produce a bright orange/red snake.

Whiteout

Probably the nearest to a completely white snake, the whiteout is a triple trait morph of amelanistic, charcoal (anerythristic Type B) and diffused.

ZigZag (Aztec)

Zigzag snakes have the left and right sides of the dorsal pattern misaligned, producing a somewhat alternating band down the back, hence the zig-zag. If the markings are completely out of synchrony then the pattern is called Aztec because it resembles the artwork of that ancient civilisation.

Top:
Sunglow
Corn snake

Bottom:
Aztec
Corn Snake

Hybrids

The corn snake has been hybridised with several closely-related colubrid snake species including the great plains ratsnake Pantherophis emoryi and the Californian kingsnake Lampropeltis getula californiae. Examples of these crosses are:

- Rootbeer snake (Corn snake x great plains ratsnake).

- Creamsicle snake (amelanisitc corn snake x great plains rat snake).

- Jungle snake (corn snake x Californian kingsnake).

Buying a corn snake

Corn snakes deserve our very best care and part of that is preparing yourself for your new arrival. If you have bought this book then this is a very important first step. Read about them. Learn what you can of their care and requirements so that there are no surprises, financial or otherwise. Once you are happy that you can care for a corn snake in the correct way, one of the most exciting parts of corn snake keeping awaits – purchasing your new companion.

There are several ways of obtaining a new corn snake, each of which has its own pros and cons.

Pet store

This is the most obvious source of a new pet corn snake, but there is a wide variation in the quality of snakes and the service that you receive. Pointers towards a good shop are:

- The obvious health of the corn snake (see later in this chapter). This can be difficult to judge because corn snakes do not always display well in shop vivaria. Inevitably they will hide behind vivarium furniture, or are curled up in a hide. Always ask to look properly at the snake.

- The provision of correct housing. This should be reasonably clean with minimal faecal soiling of the walls and cage furniture. There should be no overcrowding or mixing of species. There should, however, be some climbing and hiding furniture such as branches and artificial plants. Remember that a shop vivarium setup is different from yours at home – it is not expected that the snake will live out its lifetime in the shop. The priorities are that it needs to be readily cleanable and the snake easily caught, so a more minimalist approach is often better. Hatchlings are often kept individually in small, clear, plastic containers with one end over a heat pad.

- The shop should have plenty of ancillary equipment available for purchase, including lights, vivaria, substrates, food and nutritional supplements. Books and other helpful literature should also be available.

- Knowledgeable staff.

If all of the above boxes are ticked its probably a good place from which to buy your corn snake.

Internet

Purchasing a corn snake via the internet might seem attractive, especially as the prices are often lower than pet stores. You are, however, buying these corn snakes unseen – both the snake and it's level of care – and there is a significant risk involved. Seriously ill corn snakes may be sold to unsuspecting buyers by a small number of unscrupulous suppliers, so beware. Run an internet search on the company you are considering buying from to see if there are any comments, good or bad, about them. Regulations govern the transport of all vertebrate animals so your corn snake should be shipped to you by an approved courier and not, as sometimes happens, via parcel post.

Private breeder

Buying from a private breeder should mean that you get an opportunity to assess the health of the corn snake as well as seeing its parents and the environment it has been reared in. The quality of your corn snake will depend upon that of the breeder.

Reptile rescue and welfare organisations

It may be that some reptile rescue organizations have unwanted corn snakes available for rehoming or sale. These will have been assessed by knowledgeable individuals and there will be a significant backup in terms of expertise.

Private sale

A significant number of corn snakes are bought from private homes or acquaintances. This is the least safe means of acquiring a new corn snake

How to spot a healthy corn snake

Corn snakes can vary in their temperament. Adult and sub-adult snakes are usually reasonably amenable to being picked up and examined, but hatchlings can be very nervous. This nervousness can express itself as either frantic attempts to escape when handled, or as increased aggression. This aggression can manifest as rapid tail vibration and striking with the head. Do not be afraid – be confident and gently but firmly pick up the snake. Most hatchlings will not bite and even if they do they are unlikely to break the skin of an adult's hand.

Handling

Always ask to examine your corn snake first, and either handle it yourself or, if you are worried about it escaping or injuring itself, ask someone competent to do so. Alternatively, have it persuaded into a clear container, such as a plastic cricket carton, so that you can safely give it the once over.

Hatchlings and smaller corn snakes should be picked up gently by pushing your fingers underneath the body of the snake, allowing it to wind itself around your fingers for security if it wishes. Alternatively, keep your hands slightly cupped, with the snake in the centre of your palm. Placing one hand in front of the other will allow small snakes to continue to move forward without you having to restrain them. More nervous snakes may make an attempt to get off your hand as quickly as possible (and they can be very quick). Their actions can be controlled by gently resting your thumb on their back to slow down their progress (but you are not trying to actually restrain the snake). Do not grip or crush the body of the snake because this can easily cause bruising and serious injury.

For larger and adult snakes two hands may be needed. First of all push your fingers underneath the front third of the snake so that the 'neck' and first part of the body is supported. As you lift the snake, bring the second hand underneath the rest of the snake, or the last third or so for larger specimens. Most corn snakes will accept this happily and will often grip the hand, wrist or arm of the handler with their tail and hind end.

Many snakes will seek out warm and dark places while being handled and will attempt to make their way up sleeves, inside collars or any openings in shirts or blouses, occasionally with embarrassing results when help is needed to extract them.

Some snakes will 'taste' your skin with their tongue while being handles, using their vomerolfaction to gain more information about you. They may even learn to recognise you this way!

Give the snake a general once over. Snakes, like most animals, are symmetrical, so any obvious deviation away from this should be investigated. Lumps and bumps are likely to be abscesses or possibly tumours. In particular, if the stomach seems swollen and the snake has not eaten within the last 24 hours then be wary of the possibility of cryptosporidiosis (see page 186). Also check for areas of retained skin. These may be appear duller than the surrounding areas, or there may be raised or flaky edges. Pay particular attention around the eyes. Kinked or curved spines may indicate congenital or bone disorders.

Inspect closely for snake mites. These tiny 1mm parasites appear as black or brown dots on the snake. Typically they are found in skin folds and crevices, such as around the eyes, the corner of the mouth and the jaw, but they can be found anywhere along the body. A keen eye will spot a slightly raised scale, and next to it a mite hunkered down and partially obscured by the scale. In large infestations these mites will be so numerous that they can run off the snake on to your hands!

Look for any discharge or obvious wetness around the mouth as this can indicate respiratory disease. Snakes with serious respiratory problems will often mouth breathe, resting with their mouth partially open.

Look for tell-tale smears of mucus-like material on the inside of the vivarium glass.

If you are buying a hatchling corn snake, always make sure, or ask for assurances, that it is feeding well on frozen-defrosted pinkies. Some hatchlings are very slow starters and can be extremely frustrating to deal with.

Sexing

Sexing is relatively straightforward for adult corn snakes. Male snakes have two intromittant organs called hemipenes. When not in use these lie side-by-side along the underside of the tail, and in large males can be as long as 7.5cm (3 in). Therefore we look for the hemipenal bulges in males, just behind the cloaca. These cause a thickening of the tail in males, whereas with females the tail starts to taper relatively quickly. With hatchlings and immatures it is more difficult.

Males generally have longer tails, so if you count the scales along the underside of the tail (known as the subcaudal scales) females will usually have between 41 to 62 pairs, while males will have 65 to 86. The easiest way is to count them on an entire shed skin, but remember that this method is probably not 100% reliable, especially if the scale count is around the mid-sixties mark.

Caring for your corn snake

The correct housing, possibly more than any other factor within our control, will govern how well we look after our corn snakes.

Previously we have looked at some aspects of a corn snake's natural history and how important temperature and humidity are to snakes. These vital needs must be addressed. A corn snake will not 'adapt' if these are not correct - instead it will eventually become ill and die.

Many families have only one corn snake. They are not territorial, and neither social nor particularly anti-social, so keeping a single individual will cause it no hardship. If you do have more than one, it is probably best to keep each snake in its own vivarium.

Each individual snake can then be monitored – for example, if there is an unexpected regurgitation you will know which one it is. However, many owners become so entranced with corn snakes and the variety of colour morphs, that many owners soon end up with a sizable collection! Corn snakes can be kept together in pairs or larger groups, but there are potential problems. In view of that, here are some general recommendations on keeping groups of corn snakes together:

• Always feed each snake separately. Corn snakes can become agitated if hungry and may accidentally bite their companions. Three sets of backward hooked teeth mean that once a snake has a good grip on a prey item, it can find it hard to let go. If two snakes grab opposite ends of the same prey, it is not unknown for one individual to end up consuming the other.

• With large groups, consider providing multiple basking sites so no one animal can dominate this important resource.

• Never mix corn snakes with other species. Corn snakes have fairly specific environmental parameters and if these are not provided then they will eventually become unwell. There is also a risk of disease cross-contamination.

This rule can be bent if the vivarium is large enough (zoological exhibit-sized), the other inhabitants need a similar environment and no snake is small enough to be consumed, but most of the vivaria available to hobbyists are not suitable for this.

- Hatchlings should always be kept singly.

Here is a checklist for the minimum equipment that you will need for a sub-adult to adult corn snake.

[✓] Pet Expert: Corn snake book
[✓] Vivarium
[✓] Heat lamp/ ceramic bulb
[✓] Thermostat
[✓] Thermometers x 2 (minimum)
[✓] Hygrometer
[✓] Timer
[✓] Full spectrum light (optional)
[✓] Substrate
[✓] Hide
[✓] Shedding box (at least available when snake is about to shed).
[✓] Furniture (e.g branches)
[✓] Water bowl
[✓] Diary

Vivaria

Vivaria are enclosed, often rectangular indoor housing that come in a variety of different materials and styles. For corn snakes, surface area is of most importance, but they do like to climb too, so the vivarium should be of a decent height. For an adult snake a minimum sized vivarium would be 120cm x 45cm x 45cm high (48in x 18in x18in). Conversely, do not keep hatchlings in too large a vivarium; they appear to benefit from the security of smaller containers, possibly mimicking the microhabitats they would seek out in the wild. They sometimes appear to have difficulty finding offered prey in large, especially highly decorated, vivaria.

Corn snakes are extraordinary escape artists; they are designed to seek out, investigate and, if needs be, pass through the narrowest of gaps. This is especially true of hatchlings. Do not leave anything to chance. If it is possible for a corn snake to escape from its vivarium or container it will - it's just a matter of when!

The simplest and least desirable of vivaria are those based on an aquarium or fish tank. Although easy to find, they have poor, top-only ventilation and access that makes them unsuitable. This can also make cleaning difficult.

Puropose built reptile vivaria are much better for captive corn snakes. They are made from many different substances including wood, MDF, plastics and glass that can either be bought ready made, as flat packs or even built by yourself from scratch. The potential size and scope of a vivarium is limited only by the available space and the thickness of your wallet!

Key features of a good vivarium are:

• Access via lockable sliding doors at the front of the vivarium. This greatly simplifies routine maintenance.

• Water proofing. Fortunately corn snakes prefer a dry and warm environment, but in wooden vivaria spilled water and urine contamination can lead to rotting wood, unless the joints are silicone sealed. If doing this yourself, use a sealer designed for aquaria, not bathroom sealants that contain potentially toxic fungicides.

• Ventilation is crucial to the well-being of corn snakes. Normally ventilation is achieved by installing grids of mesh or plastic at opposite ends of the vivarium. These grids are usually positioned at different heights so that as warm air rises it exits from the higher ventilation panel while fresh air is drawn in from the lower. Some of the modern glass vivaria have mesh lids which, when combined with side-opening grills, greatly enhance airflow. There are also small fans available, which can either be connected to a timer, or better still to a thermostat, so that they are switched on when the temperature in the vivarium becomes too high.

With glass vivaria, opaque strips may need to be placed along the bottom of the sides to provide a visual barrier that the corn snake can perceive.

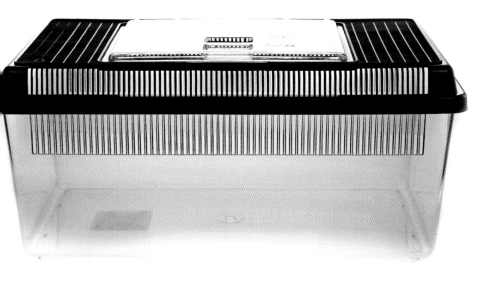

Keeping corn snakes differs from keeping many other pet reptiles, such as bearded dragons, because there is no mandatory requirement for full spectrum (with ultraviolet wavelength) lighting. However corn snakes can use UV light to make their own vitamin D3 (Acierno et al 2008). It is likely that corn snakes are able to manage without such lighting because they are largely nocturnal and have evolved to by-pass this step. Vitamin D_3 is a fat soluble vitamin that is stored in the liver, so eating whole prey, such as mice, will normally ensure a ready supply of this important vitamin.

The correct amount of heat is crucially important to reptiles and in nature this is supplied directly and indirectly by the sun. So perhaps the most difficult aspect of keeping corn snakes (and other reptiles) in vivaria is recreating the sun in the box. The sun provides corn snakes with both light and heat. Modern reptile accessories include metal halide lights that produce both light (including ultraviolet A and B) and heat, but for temperate reptiles that do not require UV-lighting, such as corn snakes, this is unnecessary and it is still more convenient to separate lighting from heating. The separation of these two key elements allows independent control where necessary.

Temperature

Keeping your corn snake at the correct temperature during the daytime is vital. Corn snakes have a preferred body temperature of around 28°C (82.4°F). Prolonged exposure to suboptimal temperatures can leave them open to secondary infections, such as pneumonia and abscesses. Night-time temperature falls will rarely cause a problem as this is what happens in the wild, in fact, a constant warm temperature is likely to be stressful to a corn snake.

In its simplest form heat can be provided by a spotlight or tungsten bulb that acts as a radiant heat source to mimic the sun. Ideally the bulb should be placed at one end of the vivarium so that a temperature gradient forms along the length of the vivarium to allow the corn snake to select the temperature it prefers. These lights should be connected to a thermostat so that the vivarium does not overheat, and to a timer so that the light is not on for 24 hours a day. Worse still is a light perpetually flicking on and off as the thermostat reacts to the temperature. To get around this second potential problem, there are ceramic bulbs available that only give out radiant heat and these are recommended. Such bulbs can provide radiant heat throughout the day and night irrespective of the lighting regime.

A less satisfactory alternative are red bulbs which produce heat and only visible red light, which is less disturbing to the corn snakes at night. Some people think that corn snakes cannot see the colour red, but this is not true; corn snakes probably have good colour vision. There are also some blue bulbs available that emit light in the UVA spectrum, also important for normal corn snake vision.

Heat mats are also readily available and these are placed either under the vivarium or on the side to provide localised warm areas; they are, however, insufficient to warm a whole vivarium and should be considered as supplementary heating only. They can help to produce a warm micro-climate under bark.

Always make sure your corn snake cannot directly touch the heat source as burns can occur. The temperature beneath the basking light should be 28- 30°C (82.4- 86°F) with a background temperature of 22- 27°C (71- 80.6°F). A night-time fall is recommended and temperatures as low as 15°C (59°F) are tolerated, even by hatchlings.

Corn snakes are largely thigmotherms. In other words they gain most of their body heat from warm surfaces, but in the vivarium this can lead to a significant risk of burns.

Never place heat mats inside the vivarium so that the snake has direct access to them.

Always place a mesh cage around heat lamps, including ceramic ones. Corn snakes like to climb and can raise as much as the first third of their body off the ground or perch to access warm surfaces – which may include the basking lamp. If the bulb is thermostatically controlled then it may be cool when the snake wraps itself around it, but on switching on, the bulb will heat up too quickly for the snake to escape, so it will burn itself. Mesh cages are commercially available.

Hot rocks – imitation rocks with a heating element inside them – should only be used with caution. Corn snakes will rest on warm surfaces to gain heat but if such 'hot rocks' are not thermostatically controlled then the risk of burning is increased. Do not rely on your corn snake having the sense to move off before it is burned. But, providing such hot rocks are on a thermostat, they can be a useful addition to the corn snake vivarium.

Lighting

Corn snakes are largely nocturnal, becoming active during the evening, although in captivity they can be active at any time of the day. As explained, they can be kept successfully without access to full spectrum lighting i.e. light with an ultraviolet A or B component. However, wild corn snakes can be active at times of day when they would be exposed to ultraviolet light, and experimentally it has been shown that corn snakes can utilise ultraviolet B for vitamin D_3 production. Ultraviolet A is probably also important for vision (and therefore how they perceive their surroundings) because corn snakes can see light in the ultraviolet range. It has been suggested that because urine will absorb ultraviolet light, snakes may use their ability to see in the UV spectrum to help identify and follow prey trails.

To give the snake a natural daily light cycle, your corn snake should either be provided with a light or be placed somewhere where there is a reasonable amount of light during the daytime, although direct sunlight should be avoided. Normally the lights should be on for twelve to fourteen hours per day, less during brumation.

If you decide to use accessory lighting, buy one of the commercially available units designed for reptiles. Typically these are fluorescent or compact tubes that have been tweaked to produce the wavelengths of light important for reptiles, as well as a light that renders more natural colouring and so appears like normal sunlight. There are fluorescent tubes that emit light in the most important parts of the spectrum, including UVB and UVA. Such bulbs are therefore often referred to as full-spectrum bulbs or lights. If you decide to use such full-spectrum lighting there are some important points to remember:

- Light intensity falls off inversely with distance from the light source, so that if one doubles the distance between the corn snake and the light tube, the intensity of the light is halved. This is important, as suspending a full spectrum light several feet above a corn snake will make its UV output of little use.

Image by
© ozzieimages
Barry Kiepe
Australia

The ideal distance will usually be supplied by the manufacturer, but if in doubt suspend the tube around 30- 45cm (12 to 18in) above the snake.

- Always position the bulb directly above your snake. Corn snakes and other reptiles have eyebrow ridges designed to keep the eyes shaded from light incident from above. Lighting from the side, especially with high UVB levels, can cause serious eye problems. Remember, snakes do not have eyelids.

- Many of these lights are rated according to their UVB output, and this is indicated by a figure at the end of the trade name. Typically these ratings are 2.0, 5.0, 8.0, 10.0 and 12.0. Each figure refers to the percentage output of UVB and so a light rated as 2.0 should produce around 2% of its output as UVB. Corn snakes should have lights rated at 2.0.

- The shape of the tube affects the area of exposure to suitable levels of ultraviolet light. The compact tubes (which resemble economy light-bulbs in appearance) produce a fairly narrow beam of ultraviolet light while the longer cylindrical fluorescent tubes emit a more even beam over the length of the tube. Ideally the tubes should extend the full length of the vivarium, but if not, position them close to the heat source so that the corn snake will be exposed to the beneficial lighting as it basks. Light intensity is so important that I recommend using at least two such tubes.

- Mesh tops can filter out up to 50% of the UVB radiation.

- The lighting is best connected to a timer so that that the corn snake has a regular day: night pattern.

- Always buy lights specifically designed for reptiles as many fluorescent tubes said to mimic the sun are colour rendered to deceive our eyes and do not emit the correct light spectrum. Unsuitable lights include those made for aquaria, general fluorescent tubes available from hardware stores and ultraviolet tubes marketed for inclusion in pond filters. These are especially dangerous as they emit UVC and can cause serious eye damage. Glass filters out UV light and so the correct tubes are made from quartz – which makes them more expensive than ordinary fluorescent lights. Unfortunately the UV output declines over time and these tubes do need replacing every 8 to 12 months.

In the past few years metal halide lighting that emits both the correct spectrum and heat have become available and work well. Combining the two obviously better mimics natural sunlight, but it does take away some of the flexibility inherent in having both functions separate. Always provide your corn snake with a hide of some sort so that it can retreat from the light should it want to.

Humidity, substrates and hygiene

Corn snakes are woodland/scrub reptiles and are tolerant of a range of humidities, so unless it is either exceptionally high or exceptionally low, humidity is rarely an issue – with one exception. During skin shedding, and the period leading up to it, the skin is more permeable to fluid loss. If the snake is in an excessively dry environment then the old, outer skin can re-attach to the new skin and cause shedding difficulties. Therefore always supply your snake with a shedding box (see page 124) and if the general humidity needs to be increased then regular misting with warm water and a hand spray should be adequate. Hygrometers for measuring humidity are available. The better ones have a digital probe that reads the humidity remotely so that the probe can, for example, be sited in a shedding box. Less useful are the disc-shaped adhesive gauges.

There is no one ideal substrate for corn snakes. The most common types are based on wood. These may be bark, wood shavings or aspen bedding. They are absorbent, so faeces and urates can easily be seen and removed as required. Avoid using with hatchlings/smaller snakes, because there is a higher risk of impaction if a piece is accidentally consumed. They also provide some environmental enrichment because, if a decent layer is laid down (2.5- 5cm [1-2 in]), then the snake is able to burrow through it.

Other substrates marketed for reptiles include coco coir, grass pellets and carpet. If you are using carpet, always have a clean, spare piece to replace a soiled one from the vivarium. If you are using natural products, remember that if they are too moist from spilled water or urine, they will harbour high levels of bacteria and fungi and can increase the risk of ill health. Always remove faeces when they are seen and replace the substrate regularly.

Cleanliness is a serious issue within the vivarium, as it is in any relatively restricted enclosure. It is very tempting to try to set up naturalistic landscapes for corn snakes, but naturalistic vivaria are harder to keep clean because urine soaks readily into the substrate and faeces can be missed.

Furniture

Furniture does not mean providing your corn snake
with a three–piece suite, but giving it things in its
environment that make a corn snake feel at home.
Corn snakes love to climb and burrow. In the wild
they are to be found under logs and man-made
structures as well as climbing into low shrubs
and rock piles, so provide structures to climb on.
Branches and rocks will also help to increase their
available exercise area, as will artificial vines and
other structures.

Hides can be provided as rocks, pieces of bark,
empty plant pots, commercially-available imitation
'dens' which are often made to look like rocks,
plastic and acrylic plants and large pieces of wood.

Another piece of furniture that I recommend is a
shedding box. The idea is to provide a safe place
with high humidity where your corn snake can shed
its skin. Ready-made ones are available, but a
functional one is easily created from a suitably-sized
plastic tub with a lid on it. Cut a snake-sized hole
into the lid and fill the tub in part with a moisture-
retentive substrate such as moss, scrunched up
tissue, or a soil/sand mixture.

If your female snake is likely to lay eggs then an egg-laying box should be provided too, although in some cases a shedding container may double as a nesting area. There should also be a water bowl.

Care of hatchlings

Many people start off with hatchling corn snakes. This is a cheaper way to acquire snakes, especially for the more sought-after morphs, but it carries a higher risk of problems. They are best kept in smaller, hygienic vivaria or ventilated containers.

Keep furniture to a minimum of a hide and small water bowl/container and keep it on paper towelling (or similar) as a substrate to allow easy cleaning. Place the container on a heat mat such that half of the base of the container is in contact with the mat to generate a temperature gradient. Check that the temperatures are suitable with a thermometer and adjust accordingly, either by using a thermostat or by altering the position of the container or vivarium. Small heat mats are available, as are strip-like ones for use with multiple containers.

Routine caring

Good husbandry of any pet involves establishing a certain routine and I recommend that you buy a small notebook or diary to keep a record of what you do. When cleaning food containers and vivarium structures, always use a commercial reptile-safe disinfectant, available from good pet stores. Never use household disinfectants such as bleach. Always keep your reptile cleaning equipment separate from your normal household materials.

Daily routine

- Check that temperatures and humidity readings are in the correct range.

- A light spraying with a hand-held spray will help to maintain a reasonable level of humidity. If possible do this in the morning, in part to mimic morning dew, but also to allow surfaces to dry and so avoid your snake being exposed to a combination of cold and wet.

- Remove any obvious faeces as you see them.

- Change paper bedding if that is in use (especially hatchlings).

- Record feedings in your diary notebook.

- Record any shedding or signs of an impending shed e.g. cloudy eyes.

VIV clean

IDEAL FOR
vivaria • bowls
work surfaces

REPTILE CARE

✓ KILLS
SALMONELLA

Cleans and disinfects
killing viruses and bacteria

Weekly

- Thoroughly clean food and water containers.

- Clean glass doors.

- Search for and remove less obvious faecal material.

Monthly

- Thoroughly clean the inside of the vivarium making sure that you remove any faeces or urates from the vivarium furniture.

- Weigh and measure your corn snake and log a record of these values in your note book.

Six monthly to annually

- Change full spectrum lights (if used) whether it appears fine or not (remember we humans cannot see ultraviolet light so we cannot tell if the bulbs are still emitting UV light just by looking). Make a note of the date.

- Replace the substrate with new.

Escapees

Snakes are born escape artists and your corn snake is no exception. If your corn snake does escape, do not panic. First try to think like a snake – look for warm, dark niches and holes that he would naturally be attracted to. Unfortunately, central heating pipes and openings in floorboards are a bad combination. Corn snakes are nocturnal so set your alarm for the early hours and you may spot your snake exploring. Corn snakes are born survivors and can go without food for many weeks if they have to, so you have time. Even if your snake escapes to the outdoors all is not lost. I have known corn snakes over-winter in the wild in the UK, turning up the next spring fit, healthy and larger than when they had disappeared the previous year. Escaped snakes do have a habit of turning up again, albeit often some two or more weeks after they disappeared.

Electrical safety

Keeping corn snakes properly inevitably involves using electrical goods. Always use suitable products designed for keeping reptiles in accordance with the instructions supplied and, if unsure, consult a qualified electrician.

Another occasional hazard is electrical tape. Snakes investigate little crevices and this can include loose ends or loops in badly-applied tape. If your snake becomes stuck to such tape **DO NOT PULL THE TAPE** – it will tear the skin. Instead, use either a good, human-safe solvent to dissolve the adhesive away, working at it gently using a cotton bud to release the snake gently. Alternatively, a well-mixed emulsion of water and olive oil can be applied to act as a lubricant.

Reference

Acierno, M.J, M.A. Mitchell, T.T. Zachariah, M.K. Roundtree, M.S. Kirchgessner and D. Sanchez-Migallon Guzman. 2008. "Effects of ultraviolet radiation on plasma 25-hydroxyvitamin D3 concentrations in corn snakes (Elaphe guttata)." American Journal of Veterinary Research, 69(2):294-297.

Nutrition

Corn snakes are carnivores. Primarily they are thought of as rodent predators, but their wild diet would also include birds and, occasionally, other small mammals such as bats. As youngsters, smaller prey items, such as lizards and tree-frogs, are taken too. Their prey items are often quite large in relation to the snake's own body size. Once a corn snake has latched on to a prey item he rapidly subdues it by wrapping his muscular body around it and constricting it. This behaviour is hard-wired into the snake, and most corn snakes will do this whether the prey is alive or dead.

As pets most corn snakes are fed on dead rodents which have been stored frozen and thawed before being offered to the snake.

Usually these are mice that have been commercially produced as food for predatory pets such as snakes and other reptiles and birds of prey. Occasionally small rats or even dead day-old chicks can be offered to vary the diet. Adult mice are pretty much a complete diet as the skeleton contains a great deal of calcium.

Nutrient content of food

Food consists of a variety of different nutritional elements that need to be considered. These add up to the quality of any given food. Good quality food provides all your corn snake requires, while poor quality food is either deficient in some or all of these aspects, or else is inappropriate for the needs of the snake.

1. Water is an essential part of the nutritional content of food. In addition to feeding the correct foods and occasional misting, clean, free-standing water should always be available.

2. Protein is needed for growth and repair of the body. In corn snakes it is likely that some is used as an energy source as well.

3. Fat is utilised reasonably well by corn snakes. Fat is needed, especially by reproductively active females as most of the egg yolk consists of fatty

materials which are an ideal store of energy for the developing embryo. Because of this, the types of fat consumed by female corn snakes may affect the viability of any eggs produced by her. Too high a fat diet (and carbohydrate) can rresult in obesity (see page 185).

4. Carbohydrates are of minimal use to corn snakes – the only ones they naturally get would be in the gut of their prey.

5. Fibre or roughage promotes normal gut motility and stool formation, both of which are vital to a normal gut environment. Much of the roughage acquired by corn snakes is in the fur and feathers on their prey.

6. Vitamins. Just like us, corn snakes require a number of vitamins to remain healthy. Vitamins can broadly be divided into water-soluble and fat-soluble. The water-soluble vitamins, such as vitamin C and the B vitamin group, cannot generally be stored and so need to be manufactured and used as needed. Fat-soluble vitamins, on the other hand, can be stored in the body's fat reserves.

The most important fat-soluble vitamins is vitamin D_3. This is required to absorb calcium out of the gut and into the body. Without it, calcium cannot be taken up in significant quantities, even if a large amount is present in the food. It is produced in several stages. First of all provitamin D is converted to a second compound previtamin D – in the skin under the presence of ultraviolet light. Previtamin D is then further converted to vitamin D_3 by a second reaction, but this is a temperature-dependant change, and so the snake must be at its preferred body temperature for this to happen. Vitamin D_3 is then further converted into more active substances in both the liver and kidneys.

Because vitamin D_3 can be stored in the liver, if a corn snake is fed on healthy mice then it will gain enough vitamin D_3 from the mice to satisfy its needs. However, corn snakes can utilise ultraviolet light to produce their own vitamin D_3 if necessary.

Corn snake food

Mice

Corn snakes are usually fed on mice which have been commercially produced and frozen. The size of the mice is up-graded as the snake grows.

Unlike wild-caught rodents these present no disease risk to either the snake or its owner. The carcasses must be thoroughly defrosted before being offered to your corn snake. The different sizes are usually referred to by their developmental stage as follows;

- **Pinkies.** New-born mice that do not yet have any hair. 1- 4g in weight. The skeleton of a pinkie is just soft cartilage; the only calcium present is in any milk in the mouse's stomach and so they should be supplemented with calcium.

- **Fuzzies or Fluffs.** These are young mice, around 4- 7g in weight. They are just beginning to develop their coats, hence the name. Again they contain little calcium.

- **Hoppers or Weaners.** These mice are around 8- 10g in size. Once weaned the mice are much more nutritious and are a more complete diet for the snake.

- **Adult mice.** These can range from 11- 15g up to 'jumbo' sizes of over 30g.

Rats

Smaller rats are suitable as food for larger corn snakes. Even smaller weaner rats are the equivalent of adult mice, at some 25- 50g.

Other rodents

Occasionally other frozen rodents are offered for sale by suppliers. Potentially suitable ones would include small hamsters, gerbils and multimammate mice (also known as African Soft-Furred mice). Never feed wild-caught rodents. These are likely to carry disease, harbour parasites, and they may have ingested rodenticides.

Dead day-old chicks

Day-old chicks are a bi-product of the poultry industry. They are the 50% of chicks that are male and therefore not needed for egg production. Like pinkies, they do not contain much calcium in the skeleton, and much of the nutrient value of the chick is in the yolk. Unfortunately the yolk is frequently rancid when the chick is defrosted and so needs removing. A vitamin and calcium supplement should be sprinkled into the cavity left by the removal of the yolk sac. Day-old chicks, at around 35- 45g, are suitable for larger corn snakes.

Practical feeding

Size of prey

Corn snakes have a distensible jaw and gullet that allows them to swallow prey items many times larger than you would imagine. However, as a general rule, offer foods of a diameter roughly equal to one and a half times that of the maximum width of the snake.

Frequency

Corn snakes, unlike the larger constrictors such as Burmese pythons (Python b. bivittatus), need frequent feeding. Adults should be offered food every 10 to 14 days. Hatchling and young snakes, which have much growing to do, need to be fed more often – every 5 to 6 days. As the snake grows feedings are progressively reduced. Pet corn snakes are quite sedentary compared to their wild ancestors and, if fed too often, can become obese, which can be life-threatening.

Offering food

Most corn snakes at the time of purchase will be feeding on frozen thawed mice of an appropriate size. The frozen mouse is placed somewhere with a reasonable ambient temperature in order to defrost. Placing frozen mice on very warm or hot surfaces may partly cook the mouse, or encourage rapid partial decomposition. If you feel you need to warm up the mouse in an attempt to encourage feeding (by mimicking a warm bodied prey) then dipping the defrosted mouse into very warm water and drying it off with paper towelling or similar works well.

Most healthy snakes will quickly learn the routine and become quite active at the first scent of a mouse, happily grabbing, constricting and consuming a mouse just laid on the vivarium substrate.

More reluctant feeders may need tease feeding. This involves trying to stimulate a feeding response by moving the prey-item in such as way as to resemble the movements of a live animal. Usually the mouse is held in a set of feeding tongs or forceps (do not hold in the hand as the snake may make a mistake and bite the wrong thing!). Such movements should be jerky and slightly erratic with the mouse at least 10cm away from the snake.

Pictured:

A range of frozen mice and rats are readily available at many specialist pet retailers. Be sure to consider the size of prey and offer foods of a diameter roughly equal to one and a half times that of the maximum width of the snake.

Remember, you are trying to arouse a hunting and striking response; if you bash the snake's sensitive nose with the mouse you are more likely to trigger avoidance behaviour.

Live foods

The feeding of live rodents or other prey items is unnecessary and risky. It is unnecessary because virtually all corn snakes can be weaned on to dead food. It is risky because mice and other rodents, if they feel hungry or threatened, can bite and seriously injure your snake. The only justification for feeding live prey is as a temporary measure to keep the snake alive whilst converting it to a diet of frozen thawed prey. The welfare of the snake must be balanced against the welfare of the rodent.

Feeding problem hatchlings

It is quite common for some hatchling corn snakes to be reluctant feeders. There are several procedures that can be attempted once the hatchling has had its first shed. Remember that rodents may not be the first prey of wild corn snakes, and this may explain why some corn snakes are reluctant to take pinkies. Also bear in mind that snakes detect potential prey items initially either by sight or by volatile scents (odours) and finally decide on what may be suitable using vomerolfaction of non-volatile scent, often taken directly off the surface of the prey animal itself.

If a hatchling corn snake absolutely refuses to feed, then the following techniques should be tried. As a general rule do not disturb the snake other than for attempted feeding. Excessive handling can severely stress a hatchling.

1. Clean a frozen, thawed pinkie with soap and water to remove the scent of the mouse. Place the pinkie by the snake's hide and leave the snake to investigate.

2. If you have access to a pet lizard, (gently!) rub the dead pinkie over the lizard or wrap some shed skin on to the pinkie. This coats it with lizard non-volatile scent particles and will change the scent. One company did make a spray on product called 'lizard maker' but at the time of writing this product is not available. Present the pinkie as above.

3. Using a set of forceps, pinch the pinkie by the hind end and move it around in a slight jerky manner in front of the hide. This teasing may trigger hunting behaviour.

4. Offer a live pinkie. It is the movement of the pinkie that one hopes will trigger a feeding response. If the pinkie is not consumed within 30 minutes, remove it and replace it with a dead one.

5. Take a seat at a desk or table as this procedure may take a little while and your arms will need support. Pick up the hatchling and hold it so that the head is gently restrained between your thumb and the curved edge of your index finger; the body is gently cupped in the palm of your hand. Gently begin to tap the nose of the snake with the dead pinkie. Please be gentle, as the nose area is very sensitive. After a few taps many hatchlings will strike and grab the pinkie. Once this happens sit very still and allow the snake to gradually ingest the pinkie. Sometimes this works just using the tail of a slightly larger mouse. Then place the snake back into its vivarium and leave undisturbed for a few days.

6. Assisted feeding. Hold the snake as above, but gently encourage the snake to open its mouth with a pinkie (or again you can use part of a slightly larger mouse, such as the tail). Start by using the pinkie to exert a gentle pressure into the middle of the mouth at its most forward point. Eventually the snake will open its mouth and accept part of the pinkie. Once the snake has a reasonable mouthful, gently jerk the pinkie back so that it catches on the hatchling's teeth. Replace and do not disturb.

Water

A shallow bowl, dish or water feature, containing clean water, should always be available.

Holiday feeding

Corn snakes, even hatchlings, will happily survive for a couple of weeks without feeding (make sure water is available) so should you go on a short holiday, feed them well for a week or two before, then leave them to it. Someone should check them on a regular basis, however, in case of problems.

Brumation

Brumation is another term for hibernation, and in corn snakes is a response to low environmental temperatures. Corn snakes, like all reptiles, are ectotherms that regulate their body temperature by behavioural means. When the surrounding temperatures drop so low that the corn snake is unable to thermoregulate properly, then they enter a state of dormancy or relative inactivity.

The fact that corn snakes brumate can be quite a surprise. Most owners are concerned about keeping them warm. After all the USA is warm, isn't it? Not all year it seems, at least in some parts of their range. While Florida, the southern extent of their natural range, has an annual temperature variation from an average of 28°C (82°F) in July and August with relatively mild winters (average of 15.5°C (60°F) for December/January), more northerly New Jersey populations must endure January air temperatures of -0.5°C (31°F).

So in the winter it can be fairly chilly for wild corn snakes, and when temperatures begin to fall consistently below around 18°C (64.4°F), this is likely to trigger brumation behaviour. Day length and possibly light intensity also probably play a part.

It can therefore be normal for corn snakes to brumate, but it is by no means essential. Normal brumation behaviour involves the corn snake going off its food, basking less and hiding away more. In the more southerly regions this may be the extent of their brumation. In more northerly areas a true hibernation may occur. In one study (Drda 1968) great plains ratsnakes hibernated from November to April in a cave in Missouri. Temperatures in the cave varied from 8.9- 10.4°C (48- 50°F). In contrast, it is likely that the southerly Lower Keys population of corn snakes are active all year round.

For breeding, best results are obtained by brumating your adult snakes. Starve them for around two weeks beforehand and wait for them to defaecate out their last meal. Then reduce the temperature to around 10- 15°C (50- 59°F) for some 8 to 12 weeks. This may be best achieved by switching off the heating at a naturally cool time of the year. If possible, also reduce day length in accordance with the seasons. This can be done by switching the lights on later and off earlier either manually or by adjusting a timer, or leaving the lights off completely and relying on the seasonal changes in incident light from outside. If the snake vivarium is in the living room then artificial lighting may counter this effect. Once the twelve weeks or so are at an end, return your snakes back to their vivarium with everything switched back to normal. Offer a small mouse after around one week and if all is well, resume a normal feeding pattern.

The change in behaviour seen with brumation can be worrying if you are not expecting it. After all, a brumating corn snake stops eating, hides away and doesn't bask, while a sick corn snake will stop eating, hide away and stop basking. If you are not sure what is going on, check these pointers:

1. Weigh your corn snake every three to four days. Corn snakes lose little or no weight during brumation.

2. Assess your corn snake. A sick corn snake will show fairly rapid signs of loss of condition, loss of muscle tone (floppiness) and may gape, whilst a brumating corn snake will appear otherwise normal and healthy with an alert appearance when disturbed.

3. Has this happened before? Check your diary – in older corn snakes did this happen around the same time last year?

Often the corn snake will end its brumation of its own accord, and once you begin to notice an increase in activity - including basking - then return to a more normal lighting and heating regime. If brumation appears to be going on for some time, and you are concerned, then you can try to reverse the process by increasing day length and upping the temperature. If this does not improve the situation, seek veterinary advice. However, if the corn snake seems otherwise fine I would allow at least two months of brumation before attempting this.

Brumation may not be straightforward. Not all individuals will routinely brumate, and this is likely to reflect their genetic inheritance, as it seems that different populations, exposed to differing seasonal winter temperatures, vary in their ability and inclination to brumate. Other corn snakes brumate no-matter what, with the urge to brumate over-riding high vivarium temperature and fourteen-hour day lengths. Brumation may be triggered inadvertently by environmental factors e.g. switching lights off early to conserve energy.

Reference

Drda W. J. (1968) A Study of Snakes Wintering in a Small Cave Journal of Herpetology Vol.1, pp. 64-70.

Reproduction

One of the joys of keeping corn snakes is the relative ease with which they can be bred. Some owners develop an interest in corn snake genetics (see the chapter on Corn Snake Morphs), and for others the production of healthy corn snakes for sale helps to off-set the costs of their hobby.

Corn snakes should have at least a 75cm (29.5in) SVL before attempting to breed from them. Some will mate without a prior period of brumation to mimic a winter rest, but to increase your chances of successful breeding, it would be best to brumate your snakes along the lines discussed in Brumation.

Make sure that your snakes are well fed. This applies especially to the female – preparing the ovaries for egg production in females occurs after brumation and can take some 5 to 7 weeks. A great deal of nutrients, including fat and other substances, will be transported into the ovaries then into the eggs to provide the building blocks for making the next generation of corn snakes.

Sexual behaviour

Courtship behaviour begins after the first, or occasionally the second, skin shed by the female after brumation is over. This releases the female's sex pheromone, to which the male will respond by chasing her and rubbing against her. Courtship in corn snakes has three parts to it - the chase, tactile alignment and true mating.

- The Chase. This begins with the male initiating courtship and ends at the first mating attempt. Female sex pheromone is picked up using vomerolfaction and stimulates the conditioned male to begin courtship. Courtship itself consists of chin rubbing, body jerks or caudocephalic waves, tail searching, pushing, nudging, and tail raising. Some males engage in gentle biting. The male will rub against the female and try to place himself over his mate, or at the very least will try to have his head, neck and the first third or so of his body over that of the female, while both snakes attempt to align their vents. The caudocephalic waves are rhythmic waves of muscle contraction that start from the cloaca and finish at the head of the male. These occur when the male is lying across the female and are thought of as providing sensual tactile stimulus to encourage mating.

It has also been suggested that in garter snakes (Thamnophis sirtalis) at least, these muscular contractions serve to compress the lung of the female, triggering a stress response that includes cloacal gaping, thus helping mating (Shine et al 2003).

- Tactile alignment. The male begins a tail-search with his own tail, attempting to align both of their tails side-by-side, which in turn aligns their cloace in readiness for mating attempts. This phase ends when intromission is achieved. The tails of both snakes will be twitching and entwining during this process. One of the hemipenes will be inserted into the cloaca of the female and insemination will occur. The male will often appear quite kinked at this point as he adjusts his position for mating.

- True mating occurs when intromission is achieved, and ends when the hemipene is withdrawn from the female cloaca. The pair, if undisturbed, will remain joined for up to twenty minutes. An insemination or copulatory plug will be left in place to help prevent other males from mating with the female. Mating occurs over many days, stopping some twenty days before egg-laying.

Mating can occur before ovulation and it seems that females can store sperm for a period of time, utilising it to fertilise their eggs only when they are ready to ovulate.

By doing this corn snakes can mate when they have the opportunity, rather than waiting for the optimum time, when a member of the opposite sex may not be available.

Practical breeding

In a well-conditioned female, ovulation can be identified by the subtle, but visible, swelling of the back half of the body as the ovaries enlarge. The ventral scales may also show more curved bulges at that point too. If not already mated, this is the time to pair her with a male.

Corn snakes should be kept separately but, realistically, it will make no difference whether you transfer the male to the female's vivarium or the other way around. If they are ready to mate, they'll go for it. Females can store sperm from previous matings and so can potentially produce clutches of mixed paternity. Once mating has been completed the pair can either be separated, or left together for a few more days to allow further matings to occur. It is considered prudent to allow males 3 or 4 days of respite before being paired with a new female. Sperm production occurs during the summer after the mating season and is stored over winter, so a given male will only have so much viable sperm available.

Where possible, remove any branches or similar furniture from the vivarium. On occasion some females may decide to wander off or climb while the pair are still joined, and in some cases this can cause damage to the hemipene of the male. Often these can be slow, or unable, to retract. In such cases, if the hemipene appears unharmed, then removing the male to a clean environment such as an acrylic vivarium without substrate, but with a hide, will often see the hemipene retracted uneventfully. If this has not occurred within a couple of hours, or if the hemipene is traumatised and bleeding, seek veterinary help. Even if amputation of the hemipene by a veterinarian is required, this is not a disaster – the male has another hemipene on the other side and so will still be able to breed in the future.

Egg laying

Depending upon whether the female was mated before or around ovulation, some 20 to 40 days after mating the female will begin to shed. By this time the eggs will be visible as a swelling of the back half to one third of the snake, and once this shed is completed she will start to look for somewhere suitable to lay her eggs. She will be looking for somewhere warm, humid and secure – somewhere

where her eggs can complete their incubation, safe from potential predators, so it is usually best to provide an egg-laying box.

An egg-laying box is much like a shedding chamber. Use a moderate sized plastic container and cut a hole in the lid sufficient for the female, with her increased girth, to enter. Use a moisture retentive substrate that will make it humid, but not wet. Moss works well; vermiculite can be used, but tends to stick to the snake. The female will enter this container and push and shove the nesting material around to create a space within which she feels secure enough to lay her eggs.

Clutches can range from as few as five eggs to thirty-five or more. Occasionally a second clutch will be laid some eight to nine weeks or so after the first.

There is little maternal care of the eggs. The female may rest up in the nesting box for a day or two, and may appear slightly disturbed when the eggs are removed. When a clutch of eggs is laid these will often stick together into a single mass and can be removed as a bunch. Healthy eggs will be soft initially, but will harden up and appear quite white or slightly yellowish with a firm leathery texture. Infertile wends tend to be smaller and more yellow and frequently do not adhere to the rest of the clutch.

Females will usually shed some ten days or so after laying and will begin to feed soon after that.

Incubation

Once a full clutch off eggs has been laid, they need to be removed within 24 hours into an incubator. Inside the egg, when it finally comes to rest, the embryo (which at this stage consists of only an aggregate of cells), gradually migrates up to the highest point of the shell so that it eventually comes to sit on top of the yolk. After 24 to 48 hours it attaches to the inner cell membrane - the allantois. This membrane is important for oxygen uptake and carbon dioxide release, calcium absorption from the shell and storage of harmful waste products. This connection is essential, but is, to start with, very fragile. Any rotation of the egg within the period of 24 hours after laying to around 20 days of incubation is liable to sheer off the embryo and cause its subsequent death.

When handling eggs always be careful not to rotate them. When removing eggs from natural egg sites to place into incubators always try to do it within 24 hours of laying and mark the top of each egg with a dot from a permanent marker pen, pencil or similar so that you always know which way is up.

Fertile eggs increase in size as the embryo develops and this can be one way of deciding whether your eggs are fertile or not. Another is by candling. This involves shining a very bright light through the egg. If there is a sizeable embryo present it will be seen as a shadow and sometimes the blood vessels lining the inside of the shell can be picked up earlier in incubation. However, often a shadow is not visible until almost the end of incubation – possibly because it is only by this point that the developing snake is dense enough to block any light. Do not rotate the egg while handling it.

Practical incubation

Corn snakes do not exhibit maternal care and fortunately, unlike bird eggs, corn snake eggs do not need to be turned, so this makes using an incubator relatively straightforward.

Commercial reptile incubators and incubator kits are available, but should you wish to make your own then any heat resistant container will do. The necessary heat source can be a small light bulb, a ceramic heater or a vivarium heat mat that is connected to an accurate thermostat. The temperature probe of the thermostat should be laid next to the eggs. An accurate thermometer is also required (to double check on the accuracy of the thermostat), plus a hygrometer to measure humidity, which should be maintained at 70- 90%. These are available from garden centres and specialist reptile outlets.

The incubator must not be permanently sealed, as some air exchange is necessary, even if this is only by lifting the lid once daily to check on the eggs. Use a small container, such as an old clean margarine tub and place some clean water retentive substrate, such as vermiculite or perlite (available from garden centres), as a substrate into this tub. Then create a shallow depression in the substrate and place the clump of eggs into it.

Place a card or other label with the morph or parental cross/I.D. and date of lay in the same tub.

Incubation periods

Eggs will incubate over a range of 21- 32°C (70- 89.5°F) which can give an incubation variation of 45 to 90 days depending upon temperature (lower temperatures give longer incubation times). However, optimum temperature is around 30°C (86°F), giving an incubation length of 55 to 60 days; 70 days at 25°C (77°F).

Apparent infertility

Adult corn snakes may be infertile for a variety of reasons. Initial starting points are confirming the sex of your breeder snakes and making sure that they are large enough to be sexually mature.

Failure to hatch/dead in shell

There are many reasons why corn snake eggs do not hatch. In the first instance consider the following:

1. Temperature. Temperatures too high or too low can lead to embryonic death

2. Humidity should be monitored and if possible a humidity of 70- 90% maintained. A very low humidity or a high airflow over the eggs can lead to an excessive loss of water from the eggs leading to dehydration and embryonic death. An egg that loses 25% or more of its weight during incubation is unlikely to hatch.

3. Oxygen and carbon dioxide levels. Remember that a corn snake developing inside the egg does breathe – not through its lungs, but across the eggshell. On the inside of the shell are membranes well supplied with blood vessels that pick up oxygen through microscopic holes in the shell and simultaneously disperse carbon dioxide the same way. In sealed incubators or in containers housed inside larger incubators, oxygen levels may fall and carbon dioxide rise to dangerous levels. Briefly opening such incubators once daily or every other day will prevent this from happening.

Hatching

Around the last week or so of incubation, the eggs will appear to collapse slightly. This is normal. Typically, within around 36 hours all of the viable eggs will hatch. There is a small "egg tooth" on the nose of the hatchling corn snake, and it uses this to wear its way through the shell, creating a slit. Often, once the shell is punctured and a small slit made, the snake may take a rest. It takes up to 24 hours for a hatchling to make its way out of the egg, but eventually a perfect miniature of the adult will emerge. Hatchlings have a total length of around 25- 30cm (10- 12in). Often the new hatchlings will group together in one area.

Occasionally some hatching snakes will appear to have trouble getting out of their shell. It is tempting to help them, but be careful. The hatchlings often have large yolk sacs still that have not been absorbed, and the blood vessels lining the inside of the shell are still functional. It is very easy to damage these structures with a serious risk of haemorrhage or wounding.

Rearing

Once feeding, the rearing of hatchling corn snakes is fairly straightforward. Please refer to the relevant sections in the chapters Caring for corn snakes and Nutrition.

References

Shine. R., Langkilde T., and Mason R.T., (2003) Cryptic forcible insemination: male snakes exploit female physiology, anatomy, and behavior to obtain coercive matings. Am Nat Nov;162(5):653-67.

Health

Captive-bred corn snakes bought from a reliable source are usually relatively trouble free pets. However, if you feel that your corn snake is unwell it is probably best isolated and kept in a hygienic vivarium where it's environment can be controlled appropriately. Ideally use only newspaper or paper towelling on the bottom so that it can be cleaned out readily, and make sure that any vivarium furniture such as hides and branches can either be sterilised or thrown away. If your corn snake is especially weak, remove any perches as it may fall, potentially injuring itself. In addition to this, the basic care for an unwell snake should include the following:

- Provision of a stress-free environment.

- An appropriate background temperature of around 26- 29°C, with a hot spot. If kept at too low a temperature a corn snake's immune system will not function correctly. Also, if your snake is on medication such as antibiotics, keeping it at its preferred body temperature will mean that its body manages and eliminates the drug in a manner predictable to your veterinary surgeon.

- Keeping the snake well hydrated is essential. Many corn snakes will lick water gently applied to their mouths with a syringe or dropper.

- It is common for sick snakes to go off their food. Assisted feeding as described under feeding problem hatchlings has its place, but should not be rushed into as it is potentially stressful and can be damaging to your snake if not undertaken correctly. For larger snakes, stomach tubing may be appropriate. If you feel that this is required consult an experienced reptile veterinarian or herpetologist.

If you have concerns it is best to arrange a consultation with your veterinarian so that your corn snake can be examined and its problems analysed and dealt with professionally. Some of the most common and most serious problems are outlined below.

Abnormal shedding

Sometimes shedding does not happen normally. This is known as dysecdysis. In most cases it is an environmental problem, and the commonest causes are:

• Low humidity. During the shedding process the skin is very susceptible to water loss and if the humidity is too low then patches of the old outer layer will stick to the new inner layer causing problems with shedding.

• No, or inappropriate, cage furniture. Snakes need something to rub against to initiate the shedding process.

• Concurrent disease. Snake mites, cuts, scars and other skin problems can cause shedding difficulties.

• Hormonal disorders. These are occasionally seen in older corn snakes.

Managing a problematic shedding involves improving the environment and some nursing care. Make sure that you provide a shedding box to give your snake a secluded, high-humidity environment in which to shed, plus a branch or stone against which it can rub. Regular misting of the vivarium will increase the local humidity too.

There are products available to aid the loosening of retained sheds and these can be tried. If there are patches of skin still attached, moisten the affected areas with lukewarm water in order to loosen the retained skin from the underlying skin. Allowing the snake to swim in a lukewarm bath will help too. Gently grasp and remove any flaps of skin but if the skin is firmly adhered, do not continue to pull. Remoisten and try again instead. If it is persistent, or if the skin is becoming bruised or damaged, stop and seek veterinary assistance.

If a spectacle (see Special Senses page 38) is retained, this is best removed using a damp cotton bud. Gentle rolling and rubbing while applying slight pressure with a damp cotton bud should eventually cause some rucking of the spectacle and allow its removal. **DO NOT PULL WITH TWEEZERS OR FORCEPS** as you risk permanently damaging the underlying cornea with a consequent loss of the use of that eye. Again, if in doubt seek veterinary assistance.

Snake mites

Snake mites (Ophionyssus natracis) can be a difficult problem to deal with. They are small (1mm), usually black or dark brown, and feed on your snake's blood. Mites tend to accumulate under the scales, around the eyes and any skin folds around the mouth or cloaca. An infested snake may spend much of his time submerged in his water bowl, except for its nostrils. Snake mites have been linked to transmitting other infections, such as septicaemia.

The main problem with snake mites is that they are parthenogenic – like aphids, females can reproduce without the need for a male – so numbers can rapidly build up in a vivaria. Treatment must therefore include the thorough cleansing of all affected vivaria. What cannot be sterilised with a mild bleach solution (5mls per gallon) must be disposed of. In addition, one should:

• Seal any joints in wooden vivaria with aquarium silicone sealer, as this is where the mites hide and breed. Do not use bathroom sealants as these contain potentially harmful fungicides.

• Replace the usual substrate with paper (changed daily).

- Wash the vivarium with warm water repeatedly, which will physically remove any mites.

- Apply topical fipronil spray (available as a flea treatment for dogs and cats) once weekly for at least four weeks. This is best first applied to a cloth and rubbed over the entire surface of the snake. Fipronil can also be used to treat the environment.

- Alternatively, consult your veterinarian for an injection of ivermection every two weeks, which will kill those that feed on the snake (note ivermectin is toxic to indigo snakes and chelonia).

- Cultures of predatory mites (Hypoaspis miles) are commercially available for use in vivaria. These prey upon the snake mites, controlling their numbers and possibly eliminating them. These are useful for complex display vivaria where thorough cleaning is not possible, or where insecticidal/acaricidal agents cannot be used.

Burns

Corn snakes gain most of their body heat from contact with warm surfaces. Unfortunately powerful unprotected heating equipment can cause severe localised burns.

This is a serious problem that you should consult your veterinarian about, as the burn will need cleaning (possibly under a general anaesthetic) and antibiotic and/or antifungal medication given. If the burns are extensive then fluids may be needed. Scarring will eventually result which may lead to localised areas of dysecdysis and, if the scarring is extensive, other problems. Restrictive scarring may mean that constricting snakes have difficulty completing the behavioural sequence necessary for normal feeding.

Flagellates

These are tiny, single celled gut parasites that can be a cause of loose stools in snakes. Under the microscope they appear as numerous motile pear-to circular-shaped protozoa. Consult your veterinarian for treatment with metronidazole.

Vomiting/regurgitation

Persistent vomiting or regurgitation can be a symptom of a wide range of problems. Make sure that the temperature is correct first, and that any prey items fed are in a suitable state to be offered. Frozen prey that has been partially thawed and refrozen may harbour bacteria and bacterial toxins that are dangerous to the snake when eventually fed. If no environmental or management cause can be found then consult a veterinarian. Other possibilities include, but are not limited to, bacterial infections, foreign bodies, tumours, cryptosporidiosis (see page 186) and other gut parasites.

Obesity

Corn snakes, especially females, are prone to obesity, largely due to over feeding. Taking prey is one of the most exciting behaviours a corn snake can demonstrate and some owners over feed to repeat the specatacle. Remember that the energy requirements for a corn snake are a fraction of that required for a similar sized mammal, because a corn snake is not expending energy keeping warm. Also, the calorie needs of a captive corn snake, with its privileged life style, is less than a wild corn would need. Obese corn snakes have a gross, swollen appearance to the body, and the head may appear unnaturally small. In extreme cases, fat may appear partially sectioned giving a 'string of doughnuts' appearance. Aim for a gradual weight loss by reducing feeding frequency or size/number of prey items. Follow the normal feeding guidelines in the Nutrition section. However, just opting for long term starvation is likely to generate serious problems however. Supplement with vitamin E to reduce the risk of steatitis (inflammation/rancidity of stored body fats).

Cryptosporidium

Crytosporidium serpentis is a real problem if it gets into your snake collection. It is a protozoal parasite, the most obvious sign of which is a grossly abnormal thickening of the stomach wall, hence it is sometimes referred to as hypertrophic gastritis. Crytosporidium causes regurgitation, extreme weight loss, depression, mucus laden stools and an obvious abdominal bulge caused by the thickened stomach.

Cryptosporidium has a direct life cycle; infection is by exposure to water containing infective cysts. It is not carried by rodents. There is no effective treatment although some regimes may help. Consult your veterinarian if you are worried about this problem. It is persistant too, with cysts remaining viable in water for up to 7 months at 15°C (59°F). Disinfect the vivarium and equipment by exposing to water above 64°C (147°F) for greater than 2 minutes. Crytosporidium cysts are very resistant to chlorine or iodine.

Bacterial infections

These are often secondary to another problem, so investigation of underlying factors should not be excluded. Typically, infections are the result of poor immunity (consider inappropriate temperatures, poor nutrition etc) or breaches of the skin, such as cuts, bites from live prey or other snakes, or mite-bites. Damp or wet environments can also lead to blisters and sores, especially on the ventral scales (known as Ventral Dermal Necrosis, Vesicular Dermatitis or Blister Disease). Septicaemias present with bruise-like haemorrhages in the skin and the snake may display abnormal behaviours. Ventral dermal necrosis appears as blisters and sores and may rapidly progress to a septicaemia. Any swelling, especially in the skin, should be considered a possible abscess. Your veterinarian will treat with antibiotics and other supportive care may be needed. Blisters and sores may need treatment along the lines of burns described above and healing of these can be prolonged. Abscesses may require surgical removal.

Stomatitis (Mouth Rot)

Usually a bacterial infection, but it can be fungal. Typically, one sees inflammation of the oral membranes that may progress to ulcers. Layers of thick pus-like material may be present. The snake may well be salivating. Occasionally, infection may track up the lachrymal duct, resulting in a sub-spectacular abcess over one or both eyes.

Snakes may not feed while suffering from stomatitis, so the snake may require fluid and nutritional support, given via stomach tube, during this time. Note that the stomach tube should be lubricated and coated with appropriate antibiotic to try to prevent spread of infection to the oesophagus and further. Topical antibiotics plus topical povidone-iodine daily may be sufficient, but surgical clean-up under a general anaesthetic may be needed.

Egg binding (Dystocia)

Egg binding can occasionally be seen in adult female corn snakes. Often it is secondary to another problem, such as obesity or lack of a suitable egg-deposition site. Distinct egg shaped swellings may be visible in the back half of the body, or it may just appear swollen.

First approaches are to provide a correct environment, including appropriate temperature, humidity and nesting chamber, to help induce normal egg laying. If this fails then consult your veterinarian, who can try to induce with oxytocin, although there is only a small window of opportunity for its effective use - within 48 to 72 hours of obvious nesting or straining seen. Do not be tempted to try to manipulate an egg out of the oviduct/cloaca – this should be done under a general anaesthetic as it is a very delicate procedure, and there is a significant risk of trauma.

Neoplasia

Corn snakes, especially older individuals, are prone to a wide range of tumours.

Salmonella

Finally some general points on salmonellosis in reptiles. These bacteria are probably best considered as a normal constituent of snake cloacal/gut microflora. They are rarely pathogenic to snakes, but excretion is likely to increase during times of stress e.g. movement or illness. In reality the risk to healthy hobbyists is minimal and infections in reptile owners are very rare. If isolated, treatment is usually not appropriate as it is unlikely to be effective long term and may encourage antibiotic resistance.

Recommendations for prevention of salmonellosis from captive reptiles issued by the Center for Disease Control in the USA are:

1. Pregnant women, children less than five years of age and persons with impaired immune system function (e.g. AIDS) should not have contact with reptiles.

2. Because of the risk of becoming infected with Salmonella from a reptile, even without direct contact, households with pregnant women, children under five years of age or persons with impaired immune system function should not keep reptiles. Reptiles are not appropriate pets for childcare centres.

3. All persons should wash hands with soap immediately after any contact with a reptile or reptile cage.

4. Reptiles should be kept out of food preparation areas such as kitchens.

5. Kitchen sinks should not be used to wash food or water bowls, cages or vivaria used for reptiles, or to bath reptiles. Any sink used for these purposes should be disinfected after use

Units & measures

If you prefer your units in fahrenheit and inches, you can use this conversion chart:

Length in inches	Length in cm	Temperature in °C	Temperature in °F
1	2.5	10	50
2	5.1	15	59
3	7.6	20	68
4	10.2	25	77
5	12.7	30	86
8	20.3	35	95
10	25.4	40	104
15	38.1	45	113

Measurements rounded to 1 decimal place.